BEAUTIFUL
Wild Animals

BEAUTIFUL Wild Animals

The long, dry southern African winter is often the best time for game-viewing because the days are cool, the bare trees offer little cover and animals have just a few places in which to slake their thirst. By sitting near a life-giving water hole, river or wetland, you can witness a panoply of wildlife in an ever-changing procession. At first light you might see the Jackal having a quiet drink after an all-night patrol; then, as the sun rises higher over the African plains, large herds of Impala, Buffalo and Zebra may start to arrive. At this water hole, Impala and Zebra enjoy a seemingly relaxed midday drink but they are wary of predators, and rightly so: Crocodile lie submerged in the dark waters, ever on the watch for an easy meal. The daytime parade reaches its climax in the cool, late afternoon, before the onset of evening, when nocturnal species take their turn.

Der lange und trockene Sommer des südlichen Afrika ist meist die beste Zeit für Tierbeobachtungen, da die Tage kühl sind, die Bäume kahl, und die Tiere nur wenige Stellen finden, wo sie trinken können. Sitzt man am Ufer eines Wasserlochs oder Flusses, kann man Zeuge einer prächtigen Tierparade werden, die in einer nie endenden Prozession am Betrachter vorbeizieht. Man kann morgens den Schakal nach seiner nächtlichen Runde trinken sehen, dann, wenn die Sonne höher steigt, tauchen große Herden an Impalas, Büffeln und Zebras auf. Impala und Zebra löschen einträchtig am selben Wasserloch ihren Durst, sind sich aber immer der Gefahr der Raubtiere bewußt. Das ist auch gut, denn der Löwe könnte im Schatten heranschleichen, und das Krokodil im seichten Wasser lauern. Am Abend kommen Nachttiere wie das Breitmaulnashorn oder der Leopard hervor.

L'hiver long et sec d'Afrique australe est souvent la meilleure saison pour voir la faune parce que les journées sont fraîches et c'est l'époque où les animaux se rassemblent aux quelques rares points d'eau pour se désaltérer. Si vous vous installez à proximité d'un de ces points d'eau, rivière ou marais, vous verrez défiler sous vos yeux un vaste éventail de la vie sauvage. A l'aurore, peut-être apercevrez-vous un chacal qui, après avoir rôdé toute la nuit, se désaltère paisiblement; puis, à mesure que le soleil monte au-dessus de vastes plaines d'Afrique, de grands troupeaux d'impalas, de buffles et de zèbres entreront en scène tour à tour. La procession animalière est à son apogée en fin d'après-midi, lorsqu'il fait plus frais et juste avant la tombée du jour, à l'heure où les espèces nocturnes telles que le rhinocéros noir, le lion et le léopard entrent en scène chacun à leur tour.

The Lion (Panthera leo) *is the largest and most powerful predator in Africa. Male and female make the perfect team: her lighter, more agile frame is well suited to hunting, while his sturdy build and ferocious appearance are vital deterrents to would-be intruders. As they patrol their territory the males emit a roar – a signal to other prides to keep their distance. The females hunt in groups, almost every night, and often specialize in a particular species. They usually crush the spine of their prey, using their powerful forelegs, before throttling the animal to death.*

Löwen sind die größten und mächtigsten Raubkatzen in Afrika. Männliche und weibliche Tiere bilden ein perfektes Team:Ihr schlanker, agiler Körper eignet sich hervorragend zum Jagen, während sein furchteinflößender Anblick mögliche Angreifer abschreckt. Löwen jagen fast jede Nacht. Das Gebrüll des Löwen ist 10 km weit zu hören, ein Signal für andere Tiere, Abstand zu halten. Die Gruppe jagt gemeinsam in Formation und sucht sich ein bestimmtes Opfer aus, das sie verfolgen. Sie brechen gewöhnlich das Rückgrat ihres Opfers mit ihren mächtigen Vorderpfoten, ehe sie das Tier zu Tode würgen. Man kann manchmal eine Löwenfamilie beim gemeinsamen Mahl sehen.

Le lion est le plus grand et le plus puissant prédateur d'Afrique. Le mâle et la femelle forment une parfaite équipe: l'ossature plus légère de la femelle convient parfaitement à la chasse, tandis que la musculature puissante et l'apparence féroce du mâle dissuadent quiconque songerait à mettre en danger la lionne et ses lionceaux. Le lion chasse pratiquement tous les soirs, et lorsque le mâle surveille son territoire, il pousse un tel rugissement que l'on peut l'entendre à dix kilomètres à la ronde ce qui met en garde les autres troupes de lions ainsi que les hyènes. Le lion et sa troupe chassent en formation et souvent choisissent comme victime une espèce particulière.

Mature males are usually evicted from the pride at about two years of age. Thereafter they form bachelor groups, roam alone or attempt to take over a pride. The last-named involves overcoming the current leader, and often the new dominant male will kill the cubs before covering the females to produce his own litters. The tenure of every dominant male is limited, and in a few years another male will take on the leader and, in doing so, diversify and strengthen the gene pool. After a gestation period of about 110 days, the Lioness gives birth to one to six cubs. Litters often drop within days of one another and the cubs benefit from communal rearing. Mortality among cubs is high, and often less than half survive.

Ausgewachsene männliche Tiere werden etwa im Alter von zwei Jahren von der Familie ausgeschlossen. Danach formieren sie sich zu Junggesellengruppen, streifen alleine umher oder gründen eine eigene Familie. Die Herrschaft eines jeden Löwen ist begrenzt, denn nach einigen Jahren fordert ein anderer Löwe den Anführer heraus; dadurch wird die Erbmasse ausgebaut und verstärkt. Nach einer Tragzeit von 110 Tagen wirft die Löwin abseits von der Gruppe ein bis sechs Junge. Die Würfe der zur Familie gehörenden Löwinnen liegen oft nur wenige Tage auseinander, und es ist für die Kleinen ein Vorteil, gemeinsam aufgezogen zu werden. Die Sterblichkeitsrate unter den Jungen ist hoch und nur einige überleben.

A deux ans environ, les mâles adultes sont évincés de la troupe et forment alors soit des groupes de mâles, soit leur propre troupe ou bien mènent une vie solitaire. Cela implique qu'ils doivent éliminer le chef actuel de la troupe et ils ont tendance aussi à tuer les lionceaux avant de s'accoupler avec les femelles pour produire leurs propres petits. La position du mâle dominant est éphémère puisque, quelques années plus tard, un nouveau mâle prendra la succession et, de ce fait, renouvellera et renforcera la composition des gènes de la troupe. Après une période de gestation de 110 jours, la lionne mettra bas, à l'écart de la troupe, d'un à six petits. Les naissances sont peu espacées et les lionceaux sont tous élevés ensemble.

A twitching tail high up in a tree is often the only clue to the presence of the shy Leopard (Panthera pardus). These elegant cats use trees as vantage points to survey their domain and as larders to store their prey. Leopards are largely nocturnal animals, and are solitary, except during breeding. The two or three cubs, which are born after a gestation period of about 100 days, have dark, woolly hair and less distinctive spots than their parents. The rosette-shaped spots of a mature Leopard serve as highly effective camouflage.

Eine zuckende Schwanzspitze im Baum ist oft das einzige Anzeichen für die Anwesenheit eines Leoparden, der scheu ist und durch sein Fell ausgezeichnet getarnt. Diese eleganten Raubkatzen nutzen Bäume als Ausguck, um ihr Terrain zu sondieren. Sie verfügen über große Kraft – es ist nicht ungewöhnlich, einen Leoparden mit einer jungen Giraffe im Maul einen Baum ersteigen zu sehen. Leoparden jagen nachts; sie sind Einzelgänger – es sei denn, sie ziehen Junge auf, dann begleiten die Eltern ihre Welpen gemeinsam.

Une queue se balançant en haut d'un arbre constitue parfois le seul indice de la présence du léopard, animal timide et habile au camouflage. Cet élégant félin s'installe dans les branches des arbres pour inspecter son territoire et pour y entreposer ses proies. C'est un animal doté d'une telle puissance qu'il n'est pas rare de le voir grimper à un arbre tenant entre ses mâchoires une jeune girafe. Le léopard est un animal nocturne et solitaire, excepté à l'époque de la reproduction où il vit en couple, ou lorsqu'il est avec ses petits.

The Cheetah (Acinonyx jubatus) is the fastest land mammal. Holding its head steady, it propels its light frame forwards with powerful thrusts of its rear legs, while its long tail whips to the left and right to balance the animal as it twists and turns in pursuit of its prey. Being capable of speeds of up to 100 kilometres an hour does not necessarily make life easy for Cheetahs: they are the most timid of the large cats, and are often chased away from kills by stronger predators before they are able to eat their fill. Cheetahs prefer hunting in the early morning or late afternoon and on account of their hunting style are usually found in grassland areas where they can attain maximum speed.

Der Gepard ist das schnellste Säugetier zu Lande. Er schnellt mit seinem Körper vorwärts, während der lange Schwanz hin- und herschlägt, um das Gleichgewicht zu halten. So verfolgt er sein Opfer. Obwohl er hohe Geschwindigkeiten erreichen kann, hat der Gepard kein einfaches Leben. Das zaghafte Tier wird oft von stärkeren Raubtieren, wie zum Beispiel Hyänen, von seiner Beute weggejagt. Geparden jagen am frühen Morgen oder späten Nachmittag, und man trifft sie in Grassteppen an, die sich für ihren Jagdstil am besten eignen, da sie dort Höchstgeschwindigkeiten erreichen können. Man kann Geparden leicht zähmen, sie waren im alten Ägypten beliebte Haustiere in den Königshäusern .

Le guépard est l'animal terrestre le plus rapide. Il se propulse en avant au moyen de ses puissantes pattes arrière, tandis que sa longue queue en mouvement lui assure un certain équilibre lorsqu'il zigzague à la poursuite de sa proie. Le fait qu'il peut atteindre une vitesse de plus de 100 kilomètres à l'heure n'implique pas qu'il ait nécessairement la vie facile: c'est le plus timide de grands félins, et des prédateurs plus puissants, tels que le léopard et la hyène, ont tendance à le chasser avant qu'il ait eu le temps de terminer son repas. Le guépard part en chasse le matin ou en fin d'après-midi et étant donné sa manière de chasser on le trouve habituellement dans la savane herbeuse où il peut atteindre une vitesse maximale.

The smallest members of the cat family reveal the same grace and playfulness as their domestic counterparts. The Serval (Felis serval) (above) patrols at night searching for food, often approaching human dwellings. The African Wild Cat (Felis lybica) (left) is slightly larger and has proportionately longer legs than the domestic variety. The Caracal (Felis caracal) (far left), with its stocky build and pointed tufts of hair growing on its ears, is a ruthless hunter which preys on small mammals.

Die kleineren Raubkatzen haben all jene Eigenschaften, für die Hauskatzen beliebt sind. Die Servalkatze (oben) streift nachts auf der Suche nach Kleintieren umher. Die Afrikanische Wildkatze (links) ähnelt der Hauskatze, ist aber größer. Der Wüstenluchs (gegenüber), durch einen untersetzten Körper und Haarbüschel an den Ohren gekennzeichnet, trifft man im südlichen Afrika an.

Tout comme le chat domestique, les félins de petite taille possèdent une grâce et un charme irrésistibles. Le chat serval (ci-dessus) part en chasse la nuit à la recherche de petits mammifères. Le chat sauvage d'Afrique (à gauche) ressemble beaucoup au chat domestique mais est plus grand avec des pattes plus longues. Le caracal (ci-contre), que l'on reconnaît à sa charpente robuste et aux touffes pointues de ses oreilles, est présent dans toute l'Afrique australe.

Hyenas have earned a somewhat unfair reputation as skulking scavengers and, while they are the garbage disposers of the bush, they are also effective hunters, quite capable of catching their own prey. Spotted Hyenas (Crocuta crocuta) (right and below) often live in abandoned termite mounds and under road bridges, and are most active after dark. They have powerful, muscled jaws and are able to chew and digest bone with apparent ease. Their whoops and chuckles are distinctive sounds of the African night.

Hyänen haben den Ruf, muffige Aasfresser zu sein. Aber sie sind auch effektive Jäger, die in der Lage sind, ihre Opfer selbst zu erlegen. Fleckenhyänen (rechts und unten) leben oft in verlassenen Termitenhügeln oder unter Brücken und sind nachts aktiv. Sie haben kräftige, muskulöse Kiefer und können mit Leichtigkeit Knochen zermalmen. Das schrille Lachen der Hyänen ist ein bekanntes Geräusch in der afrikanischen Nacht.

Le mépris dont on gratifie les hyènes est quelque peu injustifié car, bien qu'elles se nourrissent de charognes à l'occasion, elles chassent et tuent elles-mêmes leurs propres proies. La hyène tachetée (à droite et ci-dessous) vit principalement dans des termitières abandonnées et sous les ponts des routes; elle entre en activité une fois la nuit tombée. Les hyènes ont des mâchoires très puissantes et elles sont capables de broyer et de digérer sans peine les os les plus durs. Leur rire ou ricanement sinistre est caractéristique des nuits africaines.

An impish face reveals the cunning resourcefulness of the Black-backed Jackal (Canis mesomelas) (above and left). These solitary carnivores move stealthily and quietly in pursuit of their prey of insects and small rodents, and will also feed on animal remains. Black-backed Jackals are found throughout Namibia, South Africa, Botswana and Zimbabwe, and can be identified by the band of thick, dark hair which runs down the centre of the spine.

Das koboldhafte Gesicht vermittelt etwas von der Schläue des Schabrackenschakals (oben und links). Diese hundeartigen Einzelgänger schleichen auf der Suche nach Insekten und kleinen Nagetieren durch die Landschaft, und fressen mitunter auch Aas. Schabrackenschakale kommen überall in Namibia, Südafrika, Botswana und Simbabwe vor und sind an dem breiten schwarzen Streifen, der über den Rücken läuft, leicht auszumachen und zu erkennen. Sie geben einen durchdringen Schrei von sich, gefolgt von einem kurzem Bellen.

Cet air espiègle révèle un animal habile et rusé: le chacal à chabraque (ci-dessus et à gauche). Ces créatures solitaires et carnivores, qui ressemblent à des chiens, se déplacent furtivement et à pas feutrés à la recherche d'insectes et de petits rongeurs; ils se nourrissent également de charognes. Le chacal à chabraque est très répandu en Namibie, en Afrique du Sud, au Botswana et au Zimbabwe et on le reconnaît à l'épaisse touffe de poils noirs qui couvre le centre de son échine. Il émet un cri perçant suivi d'une série de jappements.

Wild Dogs (Lycaon pictus) (above and right) are currently the rarest of all African predators. The Kruger National Park is one of few areas large enough to accommodate the 450-square-kilometre home range of a pack of these animals. They hunt over great distances, snapping and nipping at the fleeing prey until it is exhausted and drops to the ground. They show refined parenting skills, standing back at a kill to give first helpings to the youngest members of the pack.

Der Hyänenhund oder Afrikanische Wildhund (oben und rechts) ist zur Zeit das seltenste afrikanische Raubtier. Der Krugerpark ist eines der wenigen Gebiete, die den 450 km² Umkreis bieten können, den ein Rudel von 10 bis 15 Tieren als Jagdgebiet benötigt. Sie jagen ihr Opfer über weite Strecken und beißen dem Tier immer wieder in Beine und Unterleib, bis es zusammenbricht. Dies hat ihnen einen Ruf für Grausamkeit eingetragen, aber sie sind sehr treusorgende Eltern.

Le lycaon (ci-dessus et à droite) est actuellement le plus rare de tous les prédateurs africains. Le Parc national Kruger fait partie de rares régions où il y ait suffisamment de grands espaces pour accueillir des meutes de dix à quinze animaux. Les lycaons couvrent d'immenses distances pour chasser leurs proies qu'ils attaquent en leur mordillant et meurtrissant les membres et l'estomac tour à tour, jusqu'à leur épuisement total. Bien qu'ils soient réputés pour leur cruauté, ils font preuve, par ailleurs, en famille de plus de délicatesse que la plupart des prédateurs.

The Bat-eared Fox (Otocyon megalotis) (left) has prominent ears which are sensitive even to the sounds of the burrowing underground insects on which it preys. Bat-eared Foxes are found usually in small family groups and occur throughout the central and western areas of southern Africa. The attractive, finely featured Cape Fox (Vulpes chama) (below) is a shy, nocturnal animal found in the drier regions of the subcontinent.

Der Löffelhund (links) hat riesige Lauscher und ein so feines Gehör, daß er die Geräusche der unterirdischen Insekten ausmachen kann, auf die er Jagd macht. Die Hunde treten meist in kleinen Familiengruppen im zentralen und westlichen Teil des südlichen Afrika auf. Der attraktive, hübsch gezeichnete Kapfuchs (unten) ist ein scheues Nachttier, das man in den trockeneren Regionen Südafrikas antrifft, wo es sich von Nagetieren und Insekten ernährt.

L'otocyon (à gauche) est doté de grandes oreilles qui lui permettent de détecter les bruits souterrains faits par les insectes dont il se nourrit. Il se déplace habituellement en petits groupes familiaux et on le trouve dans toutes les régions d'Afrique centrale, occidentale et australe. Le renard du Cap (ci-dessous), créature gracieuse et délicate, est un animal nocturne et timide qui habite les régions les plus sèches d'Afrique australe.

The African Elephant (Loxodonta africana) may weigh more than 6 000 kilograms. Despite their huge size, a large herd of Elephants can move quietly through the bush, their padded feet muffling the sounds of breaking twigs and crunching stones. A fully grown Elephant requires about 200 kilograms of bark and leaves each day to sustain its massive bulk.

Der afrikanische Elefant ist das größte Tier der Welt und wiegt oft mehr als 6 000 kg. Eine Herde kann sich trotz dieser Körpergröße lautlos durch den Busch bewegen, da ihre großen gepolsterten Füße die Geräusche der brechenden Zweige und Steine abfangen. Da die Riesen aber außer Menschen keine Feinde haben, ist ihre Prozession durch den Busch oft recht geräuschvoll.

L'éléphant d'Afrique est le plus grand mammifère terrestre du monde et il peut peser plus de 6 000 kilogrammes. Un troupeau de 30 éléphants se déplace néanmoins, malgré sa taille, sans bruit dans la brousse car les énormes pieds rembourrés de ces pachydermes étouffent le bruit des branchages cassés et des pierres foulées.

🇬🇧 *With no natural enemies except Man, a procession of Elephants is most often accompanied by the sounds of cracking branches and falling trees, which they break for food – and sometimes for fun. Ivory poachers threaten their numbers in many parts of southern Africa; the largest recorded tusks belonged to a Kenyan Elephant and weighed almost 200 kilograms.*

🇩🇪 *Sie brechen Zweige ab und reißen Bäume aus, nicht etwa nur zum Fressen, sondern mitunter einfach aus Spaß. Ein ausgewachsener Elefant braucht ca. 200 kg Baumrinde und Blätter und ebensoviel Liter Wasser pro Tag, um diese Körpermasse zu erhalten. Elfenbein ist hochbegehrt, und Wilderer sind in vielen Teilen im südlichen Afrika eine große Bedrohung.*

🇫🇷 *Mais la plupart du temps leur passage s'accompagne de craquements de branches brisées et d'arbres abattus qu'ils déracinent pour se nourrir. Vu sa taille, un éléphant adulte a besoin de consommer, par jour, 200 kilogrammes d'écorce et de feuilles et une quantité égale d'eau. L'ivoire étant très prisé, la pratique du braconnage tend à menacer les effectifs d'éléphants dans plusieurs régions d'Afrique australe.*

While Buffalo (Syncerus caffer) may be tolerant of birds such as cattle egrets, they are considered one of the 'Big Five' on account of their fearsome reputation to charge without provocation. Living in breeding herds of up to a thousand individuals, they are fiercely protective of their young. Herds have well-defined home ranges, and can usually be seen making their way to the water in the cool early morning or late afternoon, kicking up massive clouds of dust as they go. Buffalo are found in a wide range of habitats but are particularly partial to areas with abundant grasses and cover. Although they are predominantly grazers, they sometimes browse in the mopane plains of the eastern and northern parts of the subcontinent. ➤

Während Büffel sich gegenüber Vögeln wie dem Kuhreiher, der sich von den durch die Herde aufgescheuchten Insekten ernährt, sehr tolerant verhalten, zählen sie doch zu den 'Großen Fünf', denn sie sind für ihre furchteinflößenden, unprovozierten Angriffe bekannt. Herden bis zu 1 000 Tieren sind nicht ungewöhnlich, und Büffel beschützen ihre Jungen. Die Herden bewegen sich in klar abgegrenzten Gebieten, die sich selten überlappen. In der Kühle des Morgens oder Nachmittags kann man sie auf dem Weg zur Wasserstelle beobachten. Büffel trifft man in verschiedenen Habitaten an, aber sie bevorzugen Regionen mit frischem Gras. Man kann die Tiere auf den Mopaniflächen der östlichen und nördlichen Gebiete des Subkontinents äsen und weiden sehen.

Bien que le buffle fasse preuve de tolérance envers les oiseaux tels que les pique-boeufs qui consomment les insectes dérangés par le troupeau en train de brouter, cet animal fait partie des 'Cinq Grands' à cause de sa fâcheuse habitude de charger sans raison apparente. Le buffle vit en troupeaux qui peuvent comprendre jusqu'à un millier d'individus et il protège farouchement ses petits. Les troupeaux ont des territoires bien définis, qui rarement se chevauchent. On les aperçoit généralement qui se déplacent vers un point d'eau, le matin de bonne heure ou en fin d'après-midi, en soulevant des nuages de poussière sur leur passage. On trouve les buffles dans de nombreux habitats, mais plus spécialement dans les régions aux vastes étendues herbeuses.

The Rhinoceros is the second largest land mammal after the Elephant, weighing up to 1 600 kilograms. The White Rhinoceros (Ceratotherium simum) (opposite page below left and right), which has a distinctive hump on its back, is a grazer and can be distinguished by its wide, square mouth. The slightly smaller Black Rhinoceros (Diceros bicornis) (above and above right) has a hooked lip which is suitable for browsing, and is generally more aggressive and unpredictable. Rhinoceros have poor eyesight but a keen sense of hearing and smell. They favour thick bush, and mark the boundaries of their territories with droppings, creating huge middens.

Das Nashorn ist das zweitgrößte Landtier und wiegt bis zu 1 600 kg. Das Breitmaulnashorn, auch als Weißes Nashorn bekannt (gegenüber unten), hat einen deutlichen Höcker auf dem Rücken und ist ein Weidetier. Das kleinere Spitzmaulnashorn, auch Schwarzes Nashorn genannt (oben, gegenüber oben), hat eine Hakenlippe; es ist ein aggressives und unberechenbares Tier. Nashörner können schlecht sehen, aber gut hören und riechen. Sie bevorzugen dichten Busch und markieren ihr Gebiet mit ihren Exkrementen. In den letzten Jahrzehnten sind die Nashörner fast ausgerottet worden, da Wilderer die Hörner als Aphrodisiakum verkaufen. Die Zukunft der Nashörner scheint heutzutage gesichert zu sein.

Le rhinocéros est le deuxième plus grand mammifère terrestre et peut peser jusqu'à 1 600 kilogrammes. Le rhinocéros blanc (ci-contre en bas) est herbivore et se reconnaît à sa lèvre supérieure large et carrée ainsi qu'à la bosse de son échine. Plus aggressif et imprévisible, le rhinocéros noir (en haut et contre en haut), est légèrement plus petit et se nourrit de feuilles qu'il saisit avec sa lèvre supérieure pointue. Les rhinocéros n'ont pas une très bonne vue mais possèdent un sens de l'odorat et de l'acoustique très développé. Ils préfèrent la brousse dense et marquent leur territoire. Lors des dernières décennies les rhinocéros ont été menacés d'extinction à cause des activités des contrebandiers qui vendent leurs cornes.

Hippopotamus

The bulky-looking Hippopotamus (Hippopotamus amphibius) has a delicate skin which requires it to spend most of its time with only its eyes, nostrils and hairy round ears visible above the surface of the water. Out of the sun, pods of ten or 15 Hippopotamus can be seen wallowing and 'harrumphing' in the water. They do spend some time 'sunbathing', but their most important terrestrial activities take place at night, when they set off in search of food.

Das Nilpferd hat eine sehr empfindliche Haut, die das Tier dazu zwingt, den größten Teil des Tages im Wasser zuzubringen, nur Augen, Nase und Ohren über Wasser. So vor der Sonne geschützt, suhlen sie sich in Gruppen grunzend im Wasser. Flußpferde sind nachts aktiv, wenn sie auf Futtersuche gehen. Sie legen dabei bis zu 30 km zurück. Trotz ihrer behäbigen Art sind sie gefährlich, wenn sie sich bedroht fühlen – sie verursachen mehr Todesfälle als jedes andere wilde Tier.

Malgré sa forte corpulence, l'hippopotame a une peau très sensible qui ne supporte pas le dessèchement et c'est pourquoi il passe le plus clair de son temps dans l'eau avec seulement ses yeux, ses narines et ses petites oreilles rondes qui émergent. A l'abri des rayons néfastes du soleil, on peut voir des troupeaux de dix à quinze hippopotames se vautrant avec délice dans l'eau. En dépit de son apparence paisible, l'hippopotame est un animal extrêmement dangereux.

The Zebra's striking black and white markings may appear to stand out against the pale grey and brown hues of the bush, but to most predators the stripes are confusing, making it difficult to single out an individual to attack. The widely distributed Burchell's Zebra (Equus burchellii) (right, below right and far right) may be recognized by the pale brown 'shadow stripes' which run in between the darker stripes and in lacking a 'grid-iron' pattern on the rump. The Cape Mountain Zebra (Equus zebra) (below left) has a stockier build and a distinctive dewlap, and is found only in isolated areas of the Cape Province.

Das schwarzweiß gestreifte Fell des Zebras ist für das Raubwild verwirrend und erschwert deren Angriff. Ein Zebra kann einen Löwen mit seinen kräftigen Hinterläufen abhalten. Das Steppenzebra (rechts) ist an den hellbraunen Streifen auszumachen, die auf dem Rumpf ein Kreuzmuster bilden. Das Kap-Bergzebra (links unten) hat einen untersetzteren Körper und eine hervortretende Wamme. Zebras nutzen ihre Streifen, um ihre Körpertemperatur zu regulieren: In der Mittagszeit drehen sie ihr Hinterteil mit den hellen Streifen zur Sonne und senken dadurch die Körpertemperatur, morgens wärmen sie sich auf, indem sie über die dunklen Streifen das Sonnenlicht aufnehmen.

Les étonnantes rayures noires et blanches du zèbre donnent l'impression de se détacher de l'arrière-plan broussailleux aux teintes fauves, mais pour les prédateurs ces rayures sont quelque peu déroutantes et les empêchent de cibler leur proie. Le zèbre peut faire face au lion grâce à ces puissantes pattes de derrière. Le zèbre de Burchell (à droite, ci-dessous à droite, ci-contre à droite) est très répandu. On le reconnaît également aux rayures ombrées plus claires entre les rayures noires. Le zèbre de montagne du Cap (ci-dessous à gauche) est d'un aspect plus robuste; il est reconnaissable au fanon de son cou; on le trouve uniquement dans certains coins isolés de la Province du Cap.

The Giraffe (Giraffa camelopardalis) may grow to five metres in height, making it the loftiest land mammal. Their height gives them sole access to the succulent uppermost branches and shoots, but it does make drinking difficult. The arteries in the neck have special valves which stop blood rushing to the head when they bend down to drink. At water holes Giraffes are most susceptible to attack, and are therefore usually extremely nervous, sometimes taking several hours to slake their thirst. They move with long strides, attaining speeds of 60 kilometres an hour. The Giraffe's patchwork coloration darkens with age; females may be identified by the tufts of hair growing at the tops of their horns.

Mit nahezu fünf Metern Länge sind Giraffen die längsten Säugetiere im südlichen Afrika. Ihre Größe ermöglicht ihnen Zugang zu Zweigen und Trieben in den Baumspitzen, aber es erschwert das Trinken. Die Halsschlagadern haben besondere Klappen, die verhindern, daß den Tieren das Blut in den Kopf schießt, wenn sie sich zum Trinken nach unten beugen. An Wasserstellen sind Giraffen besonders gefährdet, und daher sind sie nervös und vorsichtig und brauchen mitunter Stunden, um ihren Durst zu löschen. Sie bewegen sie sich mit langausholenden Schritten und erreichen bis zu 60 km/h. Ihr Name rührt von dem arabischen Wort 'Xirapha' her, das 'der Schnellaufende' bedeutet.

La girafe peut mesurer jusqu'à cinq mètres de haut. Grâce à sa taille, elle est capable d'atteindre les meilleures feuillages situés au faîte des arbres mais, en revanche, il leur est difficile de s'abreuver. Les artères de l'encolure des girafes possèdent des valves spéciales qui empêchent le sang de leur remonter à la tête quand elles se penchent pour se désaltérer. C'est aux points d'eau que les girafes sont les plus vulnérables, c'est pourquoi elles sont aux aguets et prennent parfois un temps considérable à boire. Malgré leur air dégingandé, elles se déplacent à longues foulées et à une vitesse qui peut atteindre 60 kilomètres à l'heure. Le nom de cet animal provient du mot arabe 'xirapha' qui signifie 'marcheur rapide'.

The Black Wildebeest (Connochaetes gnou) *(right) is found throughout the open grasslands of the central dry savanna. It is also known as the 'White-tailed Gnu' because of its alarm bellow which sounds like 'ge-nu'. The Blesbok* (Damaliscus dorcas phillipsi) *(below) is found in the grasslands of the central subcontinent. Blesbok usually occur in breeding herds with one dominant male, but mixed groups are found during dry winters.*

Das Weißschwanzgnu (rechts) ist eine Antilope von eigenartigem Aussehen, das auf offenen Grasflächen und trockenen Savannen des südlichen Afrika weit verbreitet ist. Der Name Gnu rührt von dem Alarmlaut her, der wie ein gebelltes 'Ge-nu' klingt. Der wunderschön gezeichnete Bleßbock (unten) wird auf den Grasebenen des mittleren Subkontinents angetroffen. Obgleich sie gewöhnlich in Familienherden mit Leittier angetroffen werden, trifft man im Winter auch gemischte Gruppen an.

Le gnou noir (à droite) est une antilope d'apparence étrange qui est très répandue dans la savane herbeuse de toute l'Afrique australe. On l'appelle aussi le 'gnou à queue blanche'. L'attrayant blesbok (ci-dessous) est répandu dans les plaines herbeuses dans la partie centrale du sous-continent. Bien que les blesboks vivent en troupeaux, avec à leur tête un mâle dominant, on trouve aussi en hiver, des troupeaux mixtes. Quand les journées sont chaudes, ils gardent leur fraîcheur en baissant leur tête.

Kudu (Tragelaphus strepsiceros) *(above) are shy animals, and venture out of thickly wooded cover only when necessary, usually to drink alongside more frequently sighted Impala. The handsome Kudu bull (left) has large spiralling horns and is greyer in colour than the cow; outside the midwinter rutting season, they occur solitarily or in bachelor herds. Kudu are powerful antelope and can jump from a standstill to heights of up to two and a half metres.*

Die Kuduantilope (oben) ist scheu und kommt nur, wenn es notwendig ist, aus den schützenden Baumgruppen hervor. Gewöhnlich hat sie dann Durst, den sie neben der häufiger auftretenden Schwarzfersenantilope, an einem Wasserloch löscht. Der imponierende Kudubulle (links unten) hat ein großes, spiralenförmiges Geweih. Sein Fell ist eine Nuance grauer als das der Kuh. Kudus sind kraftvolle Antilopen, die aus dem Stand bis zu zweieinhalb Meter hoch springen können.

Le koudou (ci-dessus) est un animal timide et ne sort des épais fourrés que lorsque c'est nécessaire, généralement pour aller s'abreuver auprès de nombreux impalas. Le koudou mâle est splendide (à gauche); il est doté d'imposantes cornes en spirale et a une robe plus grise que celle de la femelle. Le koudou est une antilope puissante et peut sauter sans élan des hauteurs allant jusqu'à deux mètres et demi.

Larger antelope

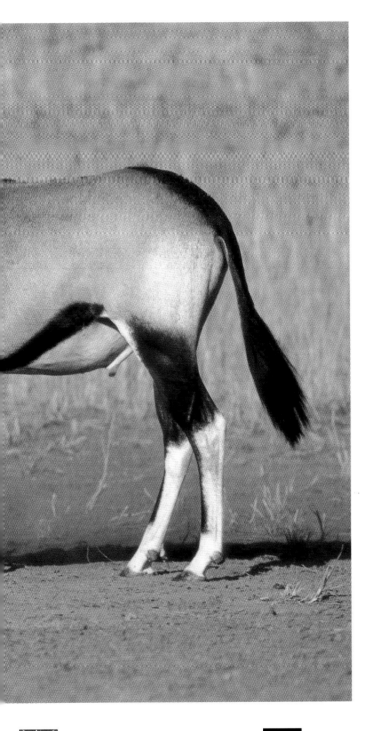

The largest of all antelope species is the Eland (Taurotragus oryx) (above right), a massive animal weighing up to 900 kilograms, which inhabits a wide range of habitats, from desert scrub to montane regions such as the Drakensberg. Few antelope are as well adapted to arid conditions as the stately Gemsbok (Oryx gazella) (above left), which is found throughout the dry northwest including the deserts of Namibia. Gemsbok have distinctive long, straight horns with striking black, white and fawn coats. Shiny black with white underparts, the Sable (Hippotragus niger) (left) has dramatic, scimitar-shaped horns which it uses to good effect against adversaries such as Lion.

Die größte Antilope ist die Elenantilope (oben rechts), ein massiges Tier von ca. 900 kg und einer Schulterhöhe von 1,7 m. Sie werden in vielen Habitaten angetroffen – von der Halbwüste bis zur Mopaneregion der Drakensberge. Wenige Antilopenarten haben sich so gut an ihre wüstenartige Umgebung angepaßt wie die stolze Oryxantilope, auch Gemsbock genannt (oben links). Man kann ihn von der nordwestlichen Region bis in die Wüste Namibias finden. Sie haben lange, gerade Hörner und ein auffällig gemustertes Fell. Die Rappenantilope (links) hat einen schwarzen Leib mit weißem Bauch und ein säbelförmiges Geweih, das sie geübt gegen gefährliche Gegner wie Löwen und Hyänenhunde einsetzt.

L'éland (ci-dessus) est la plus grande espèce d'antilopes. C'est un animal massif qui peut peser jusqu'à 900 kilogrammes. L'éland vit dans un vaste éventail d'habitats, allant des régions désertiques aux zones montagneuses telles que celles du Drakensberg. Il existe peu d'espèces d'antilopes aussi bien adaptées aux conditions désertiques que le majestueux oryx (ci-contre, en haut). On le trouve dans toute la région aride du nord-ouest, y compris la Namibie. Cette antilope se reconnaît à ses longues cornes effilées et aux contrastes frappants de sa robe noire et blanche. L'hippotrague noir (ci-contre), dont la robe d'un noir brillant contraste avec la partie inférieure du corps qui est blanche.

Smaller antelope

Springbok (Antidorcas marsupialis) (above left) *are a common sight in the northwestern regions of southern Africa. They are so well adapted to arid conditions that surface water is not essential to their survival, they extract all the moisture they need from grasses and succulents. Because of its small size, the elegant Steenbok* (Raphicerus campestris) (above right) *has to be extra cautious of predators; a precaution it has adopted is to cover its urine and droppings with dirt to remove all traces of its presence. The Grey or Common Duiker* (Sylvicapra grimmia) (left) *occurs throughout southern Africa, except in forest areas, and takes its name from its habit of diving into bush when pursued by predators.*

Springböcke (oben links) *waren einst so zahlreich im südlichen Afrika, daß die umherziehenden Herden oft eine Million Tiere zählten. Diese Wanderungen der 'Treckböcke' finden heutzutage nicht mehr in solchen Mengen statt. Die Tiere haben sich so gut an die trockene Landschaft angepaßt, daß sie kein fließendes Wasser mehr zum Überleben brauchen, und sich die erforderliche Flüssigkeit aus Pflanzen und Gräsern zuführen können. Wegen seiner kleinen, zierlichen Statur muß sich das Steinböckchen* (oben rechts) *ganz besonders vor Raubtieren in Acht nehmen. Der Ducker* (links) *kommt im südlichen Afrika vor. Sein Name rührt von seiner Angewohnheit her, sich vor Angreifern im Busch zu ducken.*

Les springboks (ci-dessus à gauche) *étaient autrefois si nombreux en Afrique australe que les troupeaux en migration comptaient des millions de têtes. Bien que les effectifs de ces springboks 'en migration' aient diminué, ce sont les animaux que l'on aperçoit le plus souvent dans les régions du nord-ouest de l'Afrique australe. A cause de sa petite taille, l'élégant steenbok* (ci-dessus) *doit prendre des précautions extrêmes contre les prédateurs. Il recouvre par exemple son urine et ses déjections de terre pour cacher toute trace de sa présence. Le céphalophe gris ou céphalophe commun* (à gauche) *est répandu dans toute l'Afrique australe, excepté dans les régions de forêts denses.*

Bushbuck (Tragelaphus scriptus) *(above) are mainly nocturnal. In the northern areas of the subcontinent they are generally coloured bright chestnut with vivid white markings, while in the southeastern areas they are a duller brown. Impala* (Aepyceros melampus) *(above right) are by far the commonest species of antelope found in southern Africa and often occur in herds of more than 100 animals.*

Buschböcke (oben) sind hauptsächlich nachts aktiv, wagen sie sich aber auch am Tag hervor. In den nördlichen Gebieten des Subkontinents haben sie meist ein kastanienbraunes Fell mit hellen Markierungen, die Tiere des Südostens haben hingegen ein braunes Fell. Schwarzfersenantilopen oder Impalas (oben rechts), sind auf dem südlichen Kontinent am häufigsten anzutreffen. Sie ziehen oft in Herden von über 100 Tieren durch die Landschaft.

Le guib harnaché (ci-dessus) est un animal nocturne bien qu'il lui arrive de sortir pendant la journée. Dans les régions septentrionales du sous-continent, le guib harnaché a généralement une robe de couleur châtaigne qu'ornent des marques blanches caractéristiques, alors que dans les régions du sud-est sa robe est d'un brun terne. L'impala (ci-dessus à droite) est de loin l'antilope la plus commune d'Afrique australe.

 *The Klipspringer (Oreotragus oreotragus)
(far left) is a nimble-footed mountain sprinter whose
skills over rocky terrain make it a match for would-be
predators such as Leopard and Jackal. The Oribi
(Ourebia ourebi) (left) is found in only a few isolated
patches in southern Africa and favours short grassland
areas, preferably with longer grasses nearby for cover.*

*Der Klippspringer (ganz links) ist ein
geschickter Bergkletterer, dessen Gewandtheit ihn in
felsigem Terrain zu einem ebenbürtigen Gegner seiner
Feinde, wie etwa des Leoparden, Wüstenluchses oder
Schakals, macht. Das Bleichböckchen oder Oribi (links)
kommt nur abgelegenen Gegenden Afrikas vor. Sie sind
sehr neugierig; deshalb sind sie eine bedrohte Spezie.*

*L'oréotrague (ci-contre à gauche) est un agile
grimpeur et sa remarquable adresse dans les régions
montagneuses en font un adversaire de taille pour les
prédateurs. L'ourébi (à gauche) n'existe que dans
certains coins isolés d'Afrique australe et préfère les
régions aux herbes courtes. C'est un animal extrêmement fureteur.*

The Okavango Delta of northern Botswana and Namibia's Caprivi Strip are home to several species of antelope that have adapted to their watery surroundings. Lechwe (Kobus leche) (right and below) are more at ease in the shallows than they are walking on land. Puku (Kobus vardonii) (opposite page above) occur widely in central Africa; in the southern regions they are found only on the southern bank of the Chobe River in Botswana. The Sitatunga (Tragelaphus spekei) (opposite page bottom) has remarkable pointed, splayed hooves which enable it to move easily in its marshy habitat.

Im Okavangodelta in Botswana und im Caprivistreifen in Namibia kommen verschiedene Antilopenarten vor, die sich an ihre wasserreiche Umgebung angepaßt haben. Letschwe (rechts und unten) fühlen sich im flachen Wasser wohler als an Land. Puku (gegenüber oben) sind in Zentralafrika weitverbreitet, aber in den südlichen Regionen beschränken sie sich auf ein kleines Gebiet, die Pookoo-Fläche. Der Sitatunga (gegenüber unten) hat ungewöhnlich spitze, gespaltene Hufe, die es ihm ermöglichen, in sumpfigen Gelände stehen zu könnnen ohne einzusinken. Sitatunga sind ausgezeichnete Schwimmer, die sich vor Raubtieren vom Land gerne ins Wasser flüchten.

Dans le Delta de l'Okavango et dans la bande du Caprivi en Namibie il existe des espèces d'antilopes qui se sont parfaitement adaptées à leur environnement aquatique. Le cob leche (à droite et en bas) est plus à l'aise dans les eaux peu profondes que sur la terre ferme. Le cob puku (ci-dessus à droite) est très répandu en Afrique centrale, mais dans les régions du sud sa distribution se limite à un petit territoire situé sur la rive sud du fleuve Chobe au Botswana. Le cob puku se reconnaît à sa taille plus petite et à son cou plus épais. Le sitatunga (ci-contre en bas) est doté de sabots pointus et évasés qui lui permettent de marcher dans les zones marécageuses.

The Warthog (Phacochoerus aethiopicus) (above and right) is known for its endearing ugliness. The canine teeth of the adults are formidable weapons used with great courage against many predators. Family groups of squeaking warthogs are often seen running through knee-high grasslands with only their upward-pointing tails visible. These 'aerials' fulfil an important function, ensuring that the young do not get lost.

Warzenschweine (oben und rechts) sind von ergreifender Häßlichkeit. Die Reißzähne der ausgewachsenen Tiere sind gefährliche Waffen, die sie mutig und oft erfolgreich gegen ihre vielen Feinde einsetzen, denn sie werden um ihres schmackhaften Fleisches willen gejagt. Ganze Familien quietschender Warzenschweine kann man oft durch kniehohes Gras eilen sehen, wobei nur die herausragenden Schwänze sichtbar sind, die dazu dienen, die Familienmitglieder nicht aus den Augen zu verlieren.

Le phacochère (en haut et à droite) est un animal adorablement laid. Les canines des adultes constituent des défenses remarquables qui sont utilisées non sans courage et parfois même avec succès contre toute une gamme de prédateurs. Il n'est pas rare d'apercevoir des phacochères en famille courant en file indienne avec la queue dressée en l'air qui émerge des hautes herbes de la brousse. C'est de cette façon que la famille reste en contact afin que les plus jeunes de la bande ne se perdent pas.

The Bushpig (Potamochoerus porcus) (below) is a secretive, nocturnal creature, preferring wooded forest areas. It is extremely dangerous when threatened, and may use its two short, razor-sharp tusks to good effect in its defence. The pig-like snout and tubular ears of the Aardvark (Orycteropus afer) (left) belie the fact that this animal does not actually belong to the Suidae (hog) family but is an anteater. It uses its claws to dig into the dirt and to scoop out its termite prey.

Wildschweine (unten) sind Nachttiere, die sich in bewaldeten Gebieten zuhause fühlen, und den Schweinen eher ähneln als ihre warzenbedeckten Verwandten. Wildschweine sind äußerst gefährlich, wenn sie sich bedroht fühlen. Das Erdferkel (links) ist ein Ameisenfresser und gehört zur Familie der Orycteropodiae, während Wildschweine den Suidae zuzuordnen sind.

Le potamochère (en bas) est un animal nocturne aux habitudes secrètes, il préfère les régions boisées. Il est extrêmement dangereux quand il se sent en danger et fait alors usage de ses deux défenses. Avec son groin de cochon, et ses oreilles longues et dressées, l'oryctérope (à gauche) est un animal singulier parce qu'en fait il se nourrit de termites et qu'il appartient à la famille des tubulidentés tandis que les cochons appartiennent à la famille des suidés.

The Chacma Baboon (Papio ursinus) *is a large primate living in family groups of up to 100 members. Grooming is important in the bonding processes of these creatures, and they spend hours searching each other for fleas and ticks. Males, which are characterized by their distinctive, dog-like muzzles and a large grey pad covering their buttocks, are ranked strictly according to status, and only the more senior members may mate with the mature females.*

Tschakmapaviane sind Primaten, die in Sippen bis zu 100 Mitgliedern leben. Körperpflege ist besonders wichtig für ihre Sozialstruktur, und morgens verbringen sie Stunden, um sich gegenseitig nach Flöhen und Zecken abzusuchen. Männliche Tiere haben hundeähnliche Schnauzen und große, graue Stellen auf den Hinterbacken. Es herrscht eine strenge Hierarchie, und nur die höherstehenden Männchen dürfen die geschlechtsreifen weiblichen Tiere decken. Sind die Weibchen läufig, haben sie ein leuchtend rotes Hinterteil.

Le babouin chacma est un primate de grande taille qui vit en groupes familiaux comprenant jusqu'à 100 membres. La toilette joue un rôle important pour l'établissement de liens; dès l'aurore, les babouins passent des heures à s'enlever puces et tiques. Les mâles qui se reconnaissent à leur museau de chien et à leur arrière-train recouvert d'un coussinet gris suivent un ordre purement hiérarchique, seuls les plus haut-placés peuvent s'accoupler avec les femelles adultes.

When in oestrus, the females show bright red pads on either side of their buttocks. Infants are born after a gestation period of six months and spend the first few weeks of their lives clinging to their mothers' undersides. Later they ride on her back and eventually they walk around on all fours. Their arch-enemy is the Leopard, and the distinctive warning bark from an alert Baboon sentry who has spotted one may be heard ringing through mountain and woodland areas.

Das ganze Jahr über werden Junge geboren und verbringen die ersten Wochen an den Bauch der Mutter geklammert. Wenn sie älter werden, reiten sie auf deren Rücken, und schließlich tollen sie auf allen Vieren umher. Ihr Erzfeind ist der Leopard. Das deutliche Warnbellen, ein 'bochom', hallt oft durch Berge und Savannen des südlichen Afrikas. Wenn Paviane durch ein Gebiet streifen, drehen sie fast jeden einzelnen Stein um, da sie nach Skorpionen und Spinnen suchen, die einen Teil ihrer Nahrung ausmachen.

L'arrière-train des femelles se couvrent de plaques rouge vif quand elles sont en cycle oestral. Les petits naissent toute l'année et passent les premières semaines de leur vie accrochés à la partie inférieure du ventre de leur mère. Une fois un peu plus grands, ils montent sur son dos et finissent par marcher à quatre pattes. Leur pire ennemi est le léopard et l'on peut souvent entendre le cri d'alarme caractéristique émis par le babouin envoyé en sentinelle. Lorsque les babouins sont passés par un endroit, toutes les pierres ont été retournées car c'est ainsi qu'ils trouvent leur ration de scorpions et d'araignées.

Walking through the bush you can often hear the soft chattering discourse of families of Vervet Monkey (Cercopithecus aethiops) as they search for fruit, flowers and leaves in the tree tops. Should you alarm them, however, be prepared for their loud, piercing scream and unnerving bark. For the most part these are very engaging animals, and their appearance is marked by their soft, grizzled pelt and striking black and white face.

Wandert man durch den Busch, so hört man oft die schnatternde Unterhaltung der Grünmeerkatzen, die auf der Suche nach Früchten, Blumen und Blättern in den Baumspitzen herumklettern. Erschreckt man sie, stoßen sie einen durchdringenden, bellenden Schrei aus. Ansonsten sind es sehr liebenswerte Tiere, die mit ihrem weichen, grauen Pelz und dem bärtigen Gesichtchen in schwarz und weiß sehr niedlich aussehen.

Si vous vous promenez dans la brousse, vous entendrez souvent le doux babillage des familles de ververts quand elles sont en quête de fruits, de fleurs et de feuilles au faîte des arbres. Si les ververts se sentent en danger, soyez prêt alors à supporter leurs cris aigus et perçants. Ce sont en général des animaux fort sympathiques et on les reconnaît à leur poil gris clair et à leur face noire et blanche assez frappante.

Bushbabies are extremely agile, climbing with great speed and jumping between trees. The Lesser Bushbaby (Galago moholi) (below) weighs 150 grams and measures just over 30 centimetres in length. The Thick-tailed Bushbaby (Otolemur crassicaudatus) (right) is almost eight times heavier and twice as large. These nocturnal primates live in groups of up to eight members but are usually seen alone.

Galagos oder Nachtäffchen sind äußerst liebenswerte Tierchen. Sie sind behende und klettern mit großer Geschwindigkeit in den Bäumen herum. Das Kleine Nachtäffchen (unten) wiegt nur etwa 150 g und ist knapp 30 cm groß, während der Dickschwänzige Nachtaffe (rechts) fast achtmal so schwer und doppelt so groß ist. Diese kleinen, nachtaktiven Primaten leben in Gruppen bis zu acht Mitgliedern.

Les galagos sont d'adorables créatures avec leurs yeux tout ronds, leur air ébahi et leur fourrure douce et soyeuse. Ce sont des animaux très agiles qui peuvent grimper aux arbres et sauter d'une branche à l'autre à toute allure. Le petit galago (ci-dessous) ne pèse que 150 grammes et n'a que 30 centimètres de haut, tandis que le galago à queue épaisse (à droite) est presque huit fois plus lourd et deux fois plus grand.

🇬🇧 *The quick-witted Mongoose has a legendary ability to kill snakes. Even the little Dwarf Mongoose (Helogale parvula) (above) dispatches small reptiles with apparent ease; like everything else in the life of this comical, bustling creature, this is done communally. The crowd pleaser of the mongoose family, the Suricate (Suricata suricatta) (right) has an inquisitive nature, and a habit of standing on its tiptoes and resting back on its tail as it surveys the area.*

Mangusten oder Mungos sind hochintelligente Tiere, und wohlbekannt für ihre einzigartige Geschicklichkeit, Schlangen zu töten. Selbst die kleine Zwergmanguste (oben) kann mit Leichtigkeit Reptilien erlegen – die Tiere jagen in Gemeinschaftsarbeit zusammen. Große Begeisterung rufen beim Besucher Surikate (rechts) hervor, die sehr neugierig sind, sich gerne auf ihre Hinterläufen stellen und sich mit dem Schwanz abstützen, um die Umgebung inspizieren.

La mangouste, petit animal vif et alerte, a la réputation légendaire de tuer les serpents. Même la petite mangouste naine (ci-dessus) se débarrasse des reptiles de petite taille sans difficulté; comme pour tout ce qui concerne la vie de cette amusante créature, cela se passe en communauté. L'histrion chez les mangoustes est le suricate (à droite); il est de nature fureteuse et se dresse sur la pointe des pieds et inspecte les environs en prenant appui sur sa queue.

The Ground Squirrel (Xerus inauris) (left and below) *feeds off nuts, insects and fruits, and is endemic to the drier regions of southern Africa. They may be recognized by the white stripes that run along either side of their body. These creatures live in complicated burrows accommodating up to 20 females and their offspring. One to three young are born after a 45-day gestation period.*

Das Erdhörnchen (links und unten) *ernährt sich von Nüssen, Insekten und Früchten, und ist endemisch in den trockeneren Regionen des südlichen Subkontinents. Diese sozialen Geschöpfe leben in verzweigten, unterirdischen Gängen, wo bis zu 20 Weibchen mit ihren Kleinen wohnen. Die Jungen werden nach einer Tragzeit von 45 Tagen geboren und kommen nach etwa sechs Wochen aus dem unterirdischen Tunneln hervor.*

L'écureuil terrestre (à gauche et ci-dessous) *se nourrit de noix, d'insectes et de fruits. Il est endémique dans les régions les plus sèches d'Afrique australe. Ces animaux communautaires habitent des terriers au réseau complexe et qui abritent jusqu'à une vingtaine de femelles avec leurs petits. Après une période de gestation, qui dure plus ou moins 45 jours, les petits naissent et émergent de leur terrier à six semaines.*

   *The Pangolin (Manis temminckii) (right) is a shy, nocturnal animal. It walks on its powerful rear legs and uses its clawed forefeet mainly for digging up its termite prey. Pangolins protect themselves by rolling into a tight, scaly ball when threatened. Hedgehogs (Atelerix frontalis) (above) are mainly nocturnal but emerge from their burrows when it rains. They are popular prey of raptors such as the Giant Eagle Owl.*

   *Schuppentiere (rechts) sind scheue Nachttiere, deren Aussehen unverkennbar ist. Sie laufen auf kräftigen Hinterbeinen und nutzen die Krallen ihrer Vorderbeine, um Ameisen auszugraben. Sie rollen sich bei Gefahr zu einer Kugel zusammen. Igel (oben) sind nachts aktiv, aber wenn es regnet, kommen sie manchmal auch am Tage aus ihren Verstecken hervor. Auch sie können sich zu einem Ball zusammenrollen.*

   *Le pangolin (à droite) est un animal nocturne et timide, dont l'apparence est tout à fait singulière. Il marche sur ses puissantes pattes de derrière et use de ses pattes antérieures qui sont munies de griffes pour déterrer les fourmis et les termites. Le pangolin se protège des prédateurs en roulant ses écailles en boule. Le hérisson (en haut) est un animal principalement nocturne mais il lui arrive de sortir de son terrier lorsqu'il pleut.*

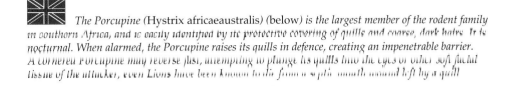

The Porcupine (Hystrix africaeaustralis) (below) is the largest member of the rodent family in southern Africa, and is easily identified by its protective covering of quills and coarse, dark hairs. It is nocturnal. When alarmed, the Porcupine raises its quills in defence, creating an impenetrable barrier. A cornered Porcupine may reverse fast, attempting to plunge its quills into the eyes or other soft facial tissue of the attacker; even Lions have been known to die from a septic mouth wound left by a quill.

Stachelschweine (unten) sind die größten Nagetiere im südlichen Afrika und gut an ihren langen, schützenden Stacheln und den rauhen Haaren zu erkennen. Wenn sie aufgeschreckt werden, stellen sich die Stacheln auf und bilden ein undurchdringliches Schutzschild. Und in Gefahrenmomenten kann sich das Stachelschwein schnell rückwärts bewegen, wobei es versucht, seinem Angreifer die Stacheln in die Augen oder andere Weichteile zu rammen; selbst Löwen sind schon an entzündeten Wunden, die von die-sen Stacheln hervorgerufen wurden, eingegangen.

Le porc-épic (en bas) est la plus grande espèce de rongeur d'Afrique australe et on le reconnaît facilement à sa carapace de piquants et à ses poils noirs et drus. Quand il se sent en danger, il dresse ses piquants et crée ainsi une barrière invincible. Un porc-épic pris au piège est capable de faire marche arrière rapidement tout en essayant de planter ses piquants dans les yeux de son aggresseur éventuel. On sait que même des lions sont morts de blessures à la mâchoire infectées suite à une attaque de porc-épic.

 Lioness and cub   *Eine Löwin und ihr Junges.*   *Lionne avec son lionceau.*

Struik Publishers (Pty) Ltd
(a member of The Struik Publishing Group (Pty) Ltd)
80 McKenzie Street
Cape Town 8001

Reg. No.: 54/00965/07

First published 1994

Edited by Ilze Bezuidenhout
German translation by Friedel Herrmann
German text edited by Bettina Kaufmann
French translation by Cécile Spottiswoode
Designed by Damian Gibbs
Cover design by Damian Gibbs
Map by Lyndall Hamilton
Typesetting by Struik DTP, Cape Town
Reproduction by Unifoto (Pty) Ltd
Printed and bound by Kyodo Printing Co (Singapore) Pte Ltd

ISBN 1 86825 729 0

Photographs © individual photographers and/or their agents as follows:

Shaen Adey p 20/21, p 41 (bottom); **Daryl Balfour** p 8/9, p 9 (top),
p 18/19, p 22 (top, bottom), p 29 (top), p 30 (bottom), p 35 (top),
p 36 (top), p 37 (bottom), p 38 (top, bottom), p 40 (top), p 44
(bottom), p 45 (top); **Anthony Bannister**/ABPL p 15 (bottom),
p 43 (top, bottom); **C. F. Bartlett** p 23 (bottom) Photo Access, p 42
(top); **Roger de la Harpe** p 4 (top, bottom), p 7 (bottom), p 9
(bottom), p 13 (top), p 17 (top), p 19 (top), p 20 (top), p 21
(bottom right), p 24/25, p 26, p 26/ 27, p 28 (bottom), p 37 (top)
ABPL, p 46/47, p 48; **W.de Beer** p 39 (top); **Koos Delport**/Photo
Access p 47 (bottom); **Nigel Dennis** front cover, p 1, p 2/3, p 5
(top), p 6 (top, bottom), p 9 (bottom left), p 11 (bottom), p 12
(bottom), p 13 (bottom), p14 (top, bottom), p 15 (top), p 16 (top),
p 17 (bottom), p 19 (bottom), p 21 (bottom left) Photo Access, p 23
(top), p 25 (middle), p 27 (bottom right), p 28 (top), p 29 (bottom),
p 30/31, p 31 (bottom), p 32 (top, bottom), p 33, p 34 (top, bottom),
p 35 (bottom), p 40 (bottom), p 42 (bottom), p 44 (top), p 45
(bottom), back cover; **Richard du Toit**/ABPL p 7 (top);
Leonard Hoffmann p 39 (bottom); **J&B Photographers**/Photo
Access p 47 (top); **Tim Liversedge**/ABPL p 36 (bottom);
National Parks Board p 39; **Photo Access** p 24 (bottom left);
Lorna Stanton p 10; **David Steele**/Photo Access p 41 (top);
A.J. Stevens p 20 (Photo Access); (top left) **Mark van Aardt** p 27
(bottom left); **Lanz von Hörsten** p 12 (top), p 16 (bottom), p 25
(bottom right); **P. Wagner**/Photo Access p 11 (top).

Front cover: main photograph *Burchell's Zebra*,
left inset *Lions*, right inset *Gemsbok*,
centre inset *Black-backed Jackal*
Title page: *Cheetah*. Back cover: *Elephant*